Nooppy's
Big lil World

Nadakkavu, Kozhikode, Kerala, 673011
www.insightpublica.com
e-mail: insightpublica@gmail.com

Title: **Nooppy's Big lil World**
Author: **Mini Benni**
Translator: **Divya**
First Edition: August 2024
Copyright © Reserved
All rights reserved.
Printed and Published by
InsightinPublica Printers & Publishers Pvt. Ltd.
ISBN 978-93-5517-717-9

All rights reserved. No part of this publication may be reproduced,
stored in a retrieval system, or transmitted, in any form, or by any means,
electronic, mechanical, photocopying, recording or otherwise,
without the prior permission of the publisher

Nooppy's Big lil World

Author: Mini Benni
Translator: Divya

About the Author

Mini Benni was born in Ernakulam. She did her schooling in Piramadom New LPS and Christava Mahilalayam Girls High School Aluva and her college in Bharat Matha college Trikkakara and Sr Teresas College, Ernakulam. She is blessed to carry a picturesque memory of her childhood that was tangled with nature.

The story was first written in malayalam, named as Loopy. Though it's a fiction Noopy the tree, Caseau the Bungalow that witnessed everything without an iota of emotion, the river nearby are all reality. As stated earlier her green childhood paved the way to the malayalam book Loopy. Ms Benni doesnt want to stop there as she is sure that her story is worth reaching a bigger crowd, joins hand with Ms Divya for Nooppy.

You can send your valuable response about the story on mini.benni@gmail.com.
9895012407

Divya

Hails from Thrissur.

Completed early education at Sacred Hearts Convent School, Thrissur.

Graduated from Government Engineering College, Thrissur.

Had a brief stint in Information Technology sector in India and moved to USA.

After a long hiatus, works as a teacher.

Loves to scribble short stories and poems both Malayalam & English.

You could send your valuable comments and feedback at divpmenon@gmail.com

Phone: +19722144875

Author's Note

"I came, I saw, I conquered" - That was Silku to me. Silku's infectious curiosity & enthusiasm makes him the sweetest, cutest & most lovable . Mini Benni has penned down Silku's love and empathy for his friends so beautifully that I felt Silku should get introduced to more non-Malayalam speaking friends too. With our dear friend, Saranya's constant encouragement & support, I started teaching Silku a new language other than Malayalam. Rest what happened is here for you as "Nooppy's big lil world".

Nooppy and her big lil world gets unveiled in the following pages in new & cool avatars - Thanks to our talented illustrator, Cyril!

I had a fun ride with Silku and his friends. I hope each and everyone of you experience the fun to its maximum.

Throughout my journey with Silku & Nooppy, my cheerleaders were Anil Sisiram, S Jayakrishnan, A P Muraleedharan, Sini A K. Without them, Nooppy would have stayed just a dream.

With utmost gratitude, I pass on my Nooppy, Silku and all of their friends to you..

-Divya.

Preface

Mrudula Ramachandran

They say, it's just a child's play to write stories for the children. For that matter, sometimes juvenile fiction is not even considered as literature.

But, to engage the little early readers, is not at all a cakewalk. It is not everyone's cup of tea. To entertain the young readers, it requires the same finesse to make someone laugh. The literature for children has to be intricately light. If creating a wonder world for the children is a herculean task in itself, how should we label the effort to translate a children's book? It takes the same effort as of renovating a house maintaining the elegance & grandeur. The wonder world has to be painted fresh in a entirely different, new language.

When I am writing about Nooppy, the first thing I could think of is 'Chuk and Gek' - the novel about two Russian kids in the snow-clad Soviet village! It conquered the hearts of millions of kids all over the world. It should not be forgotten that Harry Potter rekindled the interest in reading among kids in this smart phone era. The popularity and high acclaim of the Harry Potter shows the significance of effective translation of Junior fiction.

Coming to Nooppy, it is a book for the children and a translation work, too. The original story is beautifully written by Mini Benni. Divya has translated the story without losing the charm of the story.

Noopy is a tree at Caseu. A tree or an animal, if it talks like humans, it's always exciting for the curious minds. They become friends-at-first-sight.

The beautiful diverse world of Nooppy and her friends is purely enticing for the little explorers. Nooppy's big lil world grows into a magical kingdom in the little hearts.

Will we ever stop learning something new about nature in our lifetime? Never. If it is so, is there any other textbook for the children better than nature itself? A landscape where each and every being coexist in love and harmony - The children get to know about love and empathy at this intelligently designed landscape. All the creatures, be it a squirrel, fish, lizard, ant, bird, they all are Nooppy's friends. Nooppy's little world is thus much bigger than a human society. They watch all the human deeds and find the right and wrong in it. They get anxious over the people's negativities and cheer up ecstatic when it's all about good vibes.

Nooppy is not just a lesson about nature, it clearly marks the pandemic COVID-19 in the story.

The story depicts how the nature repaired itself when the world of humans was closed for repairs. It is not fair to comprehend the full story in the preface. I am delighted to be one of the first readers and to have this opportunity to write about it.

The author wins when every single reader connects to the story in their own ways. I am sure all the hearts will connect to Nooppy and will love Nooppy forever and ever.

Best wishes!

Contents

Silku, Curious Ever...

It was a very warm summer at 'Caseu'.

Silku, the cutest squirrel, was enjoying the day, roaming from tree to tree.

He bounced on Aamu's branches, squeaking in excitement. He practised his twirls on the tiniest twigs and hopped onto Nooppy. Nooppy carefully watched him and got unnecessarily worried. Her heart skipped a beat with each and every leap. "Be careful, Silku. Those are very small branches. You might slip and get hurt . Your mom will get mad at me then."

Listening to Nooppy's anxious tone, Aamu told her "Eey, you don't worry about Silku, dear. Do we ever have to teach squirrels about trees? Naah..Silku might still be a baby for you. But he is an independent squirrel now. Or his mom wouldn't have left him alone."

Nooppy nodded "That's true. But, Leera lost three babies before Silku. So she might be extra careful with him…"

Aamu interrupted, "Nothing like that. It's only the humans who think like this. Animals usually don't worry about their offsprings." Aamu gets too philosophical often. Nooppy loves to have such long talks with Aamu.

Caseu is the sophisticated house, painted in all white with mustard colour borders, standing tall at the end of a narrow by-lane. A grandpa and a grandma, a dad and a mom, and two kids fill Caseu's heart-n-soul with love and life.

As big as Caseu's heart, is the yard outside it too. Hundreds of plants and trees in all sizes and ages, make Caseu one of the happiest places on earth. There is Nooppy, Aamu- the mango tree, pear trees, guava trees, coconut trees, plantain trees, mangostein and many more spread all across Caseu. Caseu is the lush green mini-forest amidst the high-rising concrete jungle. Placed well inside the immensely shaded trails, Caseu doesn't sweat a single drop even in the peak summer.

Nooppy stands in Caseu's huge backyard. In full bloom, Nooppy looks amazing with bunches of pretty, fragrant pink flowers. Though Nooppy and Aamu are on different levels in Caseu's beautiful tiered landscape, their top branches meet at the same height. It's there, 'up in the air' they became the bestest buddies. They celebrate everything - the days, nights and seasons at Caseu together.

Silku was literally born into Caseu's lap. He hasn't ever been to any other places in his life. There isn't a home anywhere else other than Caseu for him.

Leaving Aamu and Nooppy, he rolled down on the palm leaf super quick and through the trees, reached the nearby pond.

Freyu went on bouncing in-n-out of the water happily and cheerfully.

"Where were you, Silku? Why didn't you come here yesterday?" Freyu shouted.

Freyu is the youngest fish in the pond. She wants to play with Silku all the time. She always dreams of racing up the trees with him and eating all the fruits. Sometimes, she tries to grab and drag him into the water to play with him. "Get in the water, dear! I will teach you to swim. We can have so much fun then." Freyu never stops to persuade him.

"Freyu, Stop moving your tail! Give it some rest. It looks so funny, your tail looks like a spring. Non-stop!!"

Freyu laughed "Dumbo, Our balance is all in this moving tail. How come you don't know that? See, you also move your tail.."

Silku didn't like it when Freyu made fun of him. Just then, he thought of his mom's words. " Do you remember that day you wanted to climb the trees with me but you didn't know how. I asked my Mom. She said you can never do that."

"Why!? Why can't I?" Freyu was devastated.

Silku blurted out "You don't have legs!"

All the other fish in the pond laughed at Freyu on this. She started to cry.

Silku couldn't handle his upset friend and so he left the pond in haste. He had some chores to do too. He paced fast to get almonds for his grandpa.

Freyu's mom, Fishi, tried to distract her and take her home. But Freyu was not at all ready to go home.

Fishi is a very sweet mother. She is the popular ' Fishma' to Freyu's friends. But now she was frustrated "Freyu, enough of this drama .. come home with me right now. I am leaving." Ignoring Freyu's tantrums, Fishi swam back home. "I hope she doesn't get into any danger. She is still learning to escape the tricky traps and yummy baits." She sighed.

Freyu had to switch-off her crying as there was no audience left. "Will go to the steps and see if those humans are there."

Through the lilies, Freyu reached the west end of the pond. She smiled at the mosses on the land and sat on the third step. She practised her ripples. "Ohh, wow! The circles are better today. I got to tell this to Mom" She was proud of her and her artistic tail.

She listened keenly to the human language. She couldn't grasp anything as they were talking too fast. She couldn't hear the full story either. Freyu was always fascinated by the stories. She wanted to stay there more. But the water there was not clear enough. Freyu felt disgusting.

She swam back home . Reaching home, she was after Fishi to know the rest of the human story. Fishi got annoyed. " I don't know any of those human's stories, Freyu. Why do you care about those, anyways? You first learn to swim properly, especially near the land. Or those same humans will snatch you and take you away from here."

Freyu was still grumpy. "I think I pampered her too much. She is getting difficult day-by-day." Fishi doubted her parenting skills.

Silku got back to Caseu. He rushed to the almond tree

through Aamu and Nooppy.

There was a thick sunshade painted in sky-blue running all across Caseu's walls to cool off the tall, glass windows. For ample air circulation inside the house, there were air holes spread across the sunshade. These air holes are usually the gateways for all the tiny little creatures outside into the grandeur of Caseu.

Though sprinting ahead laser-focused, Silku noticed a lizard peeping through one of the air holes. A metal net armed the long hole and the lizard was relaxing in his safe spot. The lizard seemed to have a pretty bad attitude and ignored Silku. It just disappeared into the dark inside in the blink of an eye. He waited some time for it to come back and then headed to the front porch.

Freaky, the white-furred cute little puppy is in the smaller kennel at the porch's right side. There is a big black dog in the big kennel on the left side. Silku doesn't know the real name of that dog, he just calls him "Blackie". Blackie never barks at him. He can identify Silku with his smell even with closed eyes.

Freaky always barks at Silku, sometimes even in his sleep too. For that matter, he barks at everyone. Once, a yellow bird was building a nest on the tree. Freaky barked for so long that the bird flew away. "How rude!?" Silku had felt then.

But, Silku likes Freaky more than Blackie. " Freaky is so cute with the beautiful black eyes. " he tells Leera often. Freaky gets to eat some yellow coloured rice daily. Somedays the food would have a foul smell. Silku hates that smell. But, he has to cross Freaky's kennel everyday to get the almonds for grandpa. There is no other way to the almond tree, too. So he just ignores the bad smell.

The thought of the unfriendly, rude lizard disturbed Silku. He paced on the sunshade for sometime and decided not to go to the almond tree. "Ahh, there goes a lizard inside the air-hole. Is this the same lizard or a different one? Do all the lizards look the same? Is there any real difference between any two lizards? Who knows? Mom might know.. Will ask her today." He was confused.

Two cars stopped at Caseu's front porch. Blackie didn't bark at the people in the cars. Freaky got excited and wagged his tail at them. "Freaky is neither swimming nor climbing the trees. Why is he then moving his tail?" Silku felt it was funny.. Probably one day he might learn from Leera or someone else - dogs wag their tails to show affection.

Silku halted at the front porch. The watchman took all the bags from the car inside Caseu. He sprints outside Caseu's gate, to the nearby corn field. " As always there would be many more squirrels in the field at this time. There is a chance for another fight like that day. I really don't know how I got into that fight. Mom was so angry at me for that. She would be mad if I got in any fights today too." He cautioned himself to avoid any fights.

At the corn field, humans were placing traps. "Ohh no, Mom had warned about the traps in the cocoa field. She said the traps are usually for us squirrels, and then rats. Why do humans have to hate us and trouble us like this? Now the traps are here too. I have to be careful not to get trapped. I have to learn so many things" He hated growing up.

The Desperate Nooppy

It was all too much bustle in the bird's nest on Aamu even late at night. It got noisy at dawn too. Aamu gets excited when the birds build nests and live on her. The chirps and tweets of any bird raises her spirits every time.

"What is so much to fuss about? It's just the birds and their lives!" Nooppy just shrugs off Aamu's zest for life.

There goes Aamu with her lectures. "Nooppy, see these baby crows, they are always hungry. They start to caw for food, in the next second they hatch out of the eggs. But, the ants, yeah the ones at my roots! Oh my goodness! You would not believe.. the baby ant, just there out from the egg, can feed on their own. It can even go and get food for the whole ant colony too. All this nature and its ways! So cool! So crazy!"

Nooppy was in awe of Aamu's observations. " I see these same things too. Birds, ants and all of this nature just like Aamu sees it. I never thought this much about their lives and life's thousand different ways in nature. My friend is a genius, for sure! She is so mature! I am truly blessed to have her as my dearest buddy!" Nooppy beamed in pride of having an intelligent friend.

"Nooppy, Do you remember I couldn't feed anything to these cute lil friends last year. What to do? I couldn't save any of my yummy fruits..These evil humans, they literally looted all my babies too early. They didn't even wait for my babies to be ripe enough." Aamu felt cheated.

"Eey Aamu, not to worry on that I think. All these baby birds and squirrels, will they ever stay hungry? After all, they just don't live only on fruits. They feed on these tiny, tiny insects too." Nooppy showed-off her knowledge.

" Hmm, you are right! I know, the mama bird feeds the young ones with tit-bits of insects, flies, and tiny fish. But, the thing is, by next season, these birds will grow big. They wouldn't get a chance to try my fruits or flowers. Maybe, If I am lucky they might be around here for my next season. Or who knows, they might feed my fruits to their babies! Isn't it crazy?Seasons go by that fast!" Aamu started day-dreaming.

In that instant, Nooppy's face dropped. "Hey dear, what's the matter? What happened? Why are you sad?"

Nooppy mumbled "Do you remember, last year when I bloomed for the first time ever! Oh my dear! Such a hearty experience. After all this long wait, I felt my life was finally fulfilled. My life has a purpose too. I felt so happy, so satisfied. But then, it was all useless. There were no butterflies, bees, no birds, nothing…" She got choked up.

" See Nooppy, you don't say there were any butterflies, bees and all. There were some. It's true that the numbers were less. Yaa..I remember the fruits were also less..It happens sometimes like that. In the first year, some trees have less fruits. You know something? You dream of happy days with lots of fruits on you, many more birds coming to you and living happily on you. Dreams do come true, my dear friend" Aamu assured Nooppy.

Silku, sitting on Aamu, listened to all these conversations. "Nooppy is sad because of less fruits, but is it really something that serious to be sad about? Maybe it's an important matter for the trees! But, why didn't the butterflies come to Nooppy? Butterflies are always here at Caseu. Did they miss Nooppy and her flowers? How would they miss something just like that? Who can I ask all these questions to? Yaa..Grandma..she will tell me the answers. Wait, how would my grandma know why the butterflies avoided Nooppy. She is also a squirrel like me. I should ask the butterflies for the reason." He decided.

He hopped onto Caseu's sunshade and looked for butterflies. There were no butterflies at all, there was a little sparrow Instead. The sparrow was enjoying it's share of nectar from the pretty red hibiscus flower. Silku squeaked two or three times. The sparrow didn't even care to look at him leaving the sweet nectar. His mouth got watered for the nectar too. He just reached the hibiscus plant and what is that he saw! There lies a very ripe, bright papaya on the ground. It was so tempting. He forgot the sparrow, the butterflies, Nooppy and everything else. He jumped to the ground. He nibbled mouthfuls of papaya and gulped to heart's content. His tummy got full with the sweet papaya. He felt happy. He looked back at the hibiscus flower. The sparrow was not there." Uh-oh, Where did it go? Where did it go this fast?" His questions stayed unanswered.

Then, all of a sudden, he felt as if someone was watching him. Some people stood there in the garden. He understood that they noticed him. He knows it is dangerous to get noticed by humans. If in such a situation, he has to move from the danger as soon as possible. He tip-toed and moved away from there.

Nooppy's despair was still worrying Silku. "Can Fishma or even Freyu help me to know about the butterflies, the birds and all those things..Eey.no.. They live in the water. How can they know about butterflies, flowers, nectar and all? Yes. The crow would know.. But the crow is always so busy with the babies. When will I see her? When can I ask her these questions? Silku was getting impatient.

The big banana flower invited him with lots of nectar and he couldn't resist it. With a tummy full of sweet nectar, he went to the coconut tree next to the plantain tree.

Silku saw Leera coming down on the coconut tree. "Till now, Mom always had answers to all my questions. She is a super-mom and a genius too. She should have solutions to Nooppy's sadness too."

Leera was happy to see Silku there. She has been longing to go onto the guava tree and enjoy the ripe, sweet guavas with him for some days now. The passion fruit vines have grown all the way up on the guava tree and there are flowers on it too now. It will be sometime for the passion fruits to be ripe enough. Leera just thought about how time flies and how fast Silku is growing up. Leera kept on looking at her baby and she couldn't believe that Silku was already three months old. Once the rains are gone and the winter is done, he will be on his own and might be with his partner too. Leera thought that she might also have a partner by that time.

Silku saw Leera on the guava tree and decided to reach there in no time. He didn't want to irk his mom once more for being slow. On the way, he remembered to check for the lizard on the sunshade. But as he reached the sunshade, Leera called him so he didn't go to check for the lizard. He had to reach Leera sooner. He planned a short-cut to the guava tree. "Go to the outhouse at Caseu's eastern side. Get on the mangostein tree behind the outhouse & the guava tree is next to it."

At the outhouse, he saw some people going towards Nooppy. "Why are they going to Nooppy?" He squeaked loudly, lost in his thoughts. One person stared at him on the squeak. He fled from there with fear and landed on the guava tree.

The people who came had plans to build something at Nooppy's place. One of them inspected Nooppy, her height, her strength, the trunk, the branches and everything. Nooppy was anxious about all the happenings around her. Aamu could sense Nooppy's distress. She forcefully dropped one of her dried branches from the top. The people got distracted with the loud thud. Leaving Nooppy alone, they left from there. Aamu, swayed hard and whistled for the wind to cheer up Nooppy. Aamu tried to swing closer and hug Nooppy tighter.

The sky was calm and azure. Clouds started flowing in and the sky too started pouring down on Nooppy. Nooppy got drenched in the pitter-patter summer rain and cooled off, but Aamu could still feel the lingering despair in Nooppy.

It's not that the trees don't understand the human mindset. They agree to the point that the trees are meant to bear fruits. People are never happy with just the cool shade from Nooppy, they want fruits from her, that too in bunches. There is no use in growing a tree for nothing. In the severe pain of failure, Nooppy's roots tightened themselves around the soil, yearning for some more life.

Nooppy was always well taken care of. Water, in surplus, from Caseu's kitchen and washrooms were all directed to Nooppy. Nooppy was happy and grateful for the care she gets. But now, Nooppy feels she is a wasteful life. She just takes up space with this humongous trunk. She looked at the lush green leaves. "They are beautiful..but why are there no fruits?" She cried hard in the rain.

Silku and Leera returned to their nest when the rain got heavy. Silku is seeing such heavy rain for the first time in his life. He looked up at the sky." Where does the sky store this much water? Why is it all pouring down now? Does it rain in the pond too? Can Freyu also see the rain when she is in the water? Will the fish go below the water, to their houses, when it rains? What will Nooppy and Aamu do in the rain? Where will they go to escape the rain? "His questions were also unstoppable just like the rain. Silku hoped Nooppy would be happy after the rains. Even then he wanted to talk to his mom about Nooppy being sad all the time.

Silku wondered about the nature around him. He was

always fascinated by the sun, bright sunlight, rain, dewdrops, days, nights and so many other things. He felt there would always be more to know and experience about the amazing nature.

There would always be lots of guests at Caseu. Nooppy got more water than usual. "Some guests are at Caseu today. There should be some celebrations going on". Nooppy told Aamu. "The hosts should be so nice for the guests to feel welcomed here. We are so blessed to have the people at Caseu as our owners."

Caseu and surroundings stayed pleasantly moist even after the rains. Silku was happy to see Caseu after the rains. "Where did everyone go when it rained? Where are the birds, butterflies, ants? Are they still hiding? Where are they hiding? Silku was still surprised about the rain. Silku roamed all around the wet leaves at Caseu.

The Warrior Roach

The rambutan tree behind Blackie's dog-house was full of ripe fruits at that time of the year. The Caseu people have covered the tree with a big net to save the sweet fruits from Silku and his friends. Silku but still went on the tree daily to try his luck.

Sitting on the rambutan tree, Silku saw three cars going out of the Caseu's gate.Seeing the rambutan fruits, Silku thought of Nooppy. "Why didn't they cover Nooppy like this? Mom was saying Nooppy didn't get enough good food, so she had less fruits. This tree has so many fruits. So, how did this tree get the good food from?"

"Ohh, I still have to gather some more food before the rainy season. I have to start getting pea-pods from the fields today. It will take some trips back - n - forth to fill enough pea-pods in the burrow for the season. It would have been so easy if I had a bigger mouth. I could carry more pea-pods in one go."

Silku wanted to check on Nooppy. He took the route through the pear tree. It's easier to cross Caseu this way to reach Nooppy. Though he was rushing as always, he noticed something under the pear tree. Some roaches lay upside down under the pear tree. There were three or four of them. One tried to move its legs, all the others seemed to be dead. Silku tip-toed to the live roach. "Is it trying to say something? Is it asking for water? Why would it need water when it's already wet in the rain?"

He saw some rain water sparkling in a flower-petal nearby. He brought that petal to the roach. Just then, a gentle breeze made the raindrops drizzle down the leaves. The roach rose back to life with that spray of energy.

Silku got curious. The roach still choked on something. He gasped for air. "Do you know how many dark, humid spots are there inside Caseu? We could easily thrive there. But those mean househelps never let us stay there. It's because of only those cruel people, I am dying. I learnt about this hazard long back. I feared this would happen sooner than expected. You know, we had organised an awareness seminar for our young friends about this danger. The cleaning liquids and sprays loaded with strong scents made us this sick. "He took his last breath and his words of caution vanished into thin air.

The roach mostly fed on the thick, heavy books in Caseu. So he always thought and spoke like an intellectual.. Silku didn't understand a single word from what the roach muttered. But he was now sure that there are many more hidden dangers in Caseu.

Silku glanced over Caseu from the pear tree. " Will I die like the roach too if I go inside this dangerous place?" He looked around. "Nature is so warm and safe. I can wander anywhere outside Caseu without any fear."

Reaching Nooppy, Silku played on her for some time. He really wished to cheer Nooppy up.

Aamu was in deep thoughts to even notice Leera was on her. With Leera's loud squeak, Aamu woke up from her overthinking. Silku saw Leera on Aamu. "Now, Mom will not let me hop around. Let me go to the pond then. Have to talk to Freyu about the rain too."

He saw a rat running around near the pond. That was Eleema's child. He was confused if that was the elder one or the youngest one. All of Eleema's kids looked the same.

The rat disappeared into its hole, but immediately stepped out and walked towards him. He thought of calling him Ratus. But he didn't respond to his new name. He went inside the hole again. Silku waited for Ratus, but Eleema came out of the hole and smiled at him. Leera and Eleema knew each other. Some days back, Eleema had warned Leera about the traps in the cocoa field. Silku always found humans strange. "There is food in nature for all living beings. But then why do these humans want to harm the animals?"

Silku was upset as Ratus didn't talk to him. "Somehow, I don't like him either. Is it because he doesn't live in the trees? No, it could not be the reason. Freyu, Fishma live in water and there are other friends who don't live on trees. I like them all. It's ok. Mom always says to be nice to everyone. I should be nice to Ratus too from next time." When Eleema went into a hole, Silku returned to Caseu. "Uh, Missed to see Freyu. Never mind. Will meet her tomorrow. ''

A caterpillar was chewing in the leaves on the lemon tree. Silku never went to that tree, as there are tiny thorns on it. He recently learnt that the butterflies lay eggs under the leaves. The caterpillars hatch out of the eggs in four or five days. The caterpillar feeds on the tiny leaf sprouts on the trees for days. The leaves guard it from the birds too. A person came out from Caseu and plucked some yellow lemons from the tree. "What if that person saw the caterpillar there on the leaf? He would have squeezed it to death and destroyed the leaf itself. No wonder, the caterpillar is green as the leaf. It knows how to be safe for sure. How clever is the caterpillar!" Silku was amazed.

The big taro leaf was happy, playing with the raindrops stuck inside it. Flies were fluttering in and around the droplets.

Caseu got all cosy after the rains. It sure was more beautiful than before.

Alberto's Team

"The ants are so disciplined," Aamu told Alberto, the leader of the ant colony at Caseu. "There would be around millions of ants in a single colony. Am I right, Alberto? All the colonies function in a strict organisation pattern. There would be queen-ants laying eggs just responsible for progeneration, an army, some servants, ants with wings, male and female ants and much more." Aamu kept on wondering about the ant lives. "Tell me one thing, Alberto. Why are you not building any colonies at Nooppy's roots? Is there any danger there?"

Aamu repeated the question and Alberto ignored it again. Alberto stood tall on Aamu's roots and carefully analysed Nooppy . "Can you see Aamu, the soil is too moist at Nooppy's. There are some unidentifiable pungent smells too. We ants follow strict rules to build new colonies. Rules are rules. No compromise on that. It's the matter of life-n-death."

Alberto monitored his busy team-mates. He felt proud of them. "They don't have to be supervised regularly. They all work so efficiently without any constant reminders. They keep the colonies so clean and organised. Anyways, Aamu didn't pressure me to build a colony at Nooppy's. That's a huge relief." He took a deep sigh and resumed his daily grind.

Alberto couldn't stop thinking of Caseu though. He always had a huge craving for all the sweet smells from that humongous castle. But there's something more to it. There are some suffocating strong smells too. That's why we haven't completely invaded Caseu till now. Yaa, it's true that some of us had been there at Caseu. We have lost some of them too. Revolt is in our veins. We can't stop that. We shall overcome any challenges." Alberto re-assured himself.

Nooppy always tries to engage in something. She keeps tabs on the guests at Caseu daily and reports to Aamu. Aamu understands Nooppy is just distracting herself from unwanted thoughts. Over the years, Aamu has learnt one more thing. The more flexible trees are, the longer they can stand tall.Just then the parrots flew past Aamu from the coconut tree. Aamu recognised those parrots. " They were so little. See, they grew up so fast and now they learnt to fly too. How ironic things are. The woodpeckers come and poke holes in the trees. But, do we ever complain?We love everyone with our soul. These woodpeckers have a great sense of which tree to choose and all. They leave the holes once they are done with the eggs and baby birds. Some other birds come and occupy the holes later. This time, it is the parrot. See, parrots are smart too. They know they are soft and they will never be able to poke holes and make nests. It's usually around three or four eggs at a time for the parrots. Most of the parrots would be on their own by the rainy season. It's all give & take in nature. Everyone co-exist peacefully."

Aamu looked around at all the grass, the small plants, the creepers, the big plants and huge trees at Caseu. " Its true plants can't move or communicate. But we all are so emotional. What will humans do without us? What would animals do if we weren't there? Most of them feed on us. We should be proud we make any land beautiful where we are planted."

It's always friendships that matter. Aamu felt blessed to have Nooppy with her. Aamu listens to her and understands her emotions more than anyone else. But sometimes, Nooppy thinks too much and gets desperate. Aamu tells her to always hope for the best. Nooppy is very lovely and caring. Why should someone with a kind soul and good heart worry? Whatever happens, it would always be in their best interest.

Afterall, life is all about the little little things.

Nooppy at Risk

"Silku is not here these days. why is he not coming here, Aamu?"

"I really don't know, maybe because there are no fruits for him here. And, he is a big boy now. He has to search for his girlfriend too." Aamu winked at Nooppy.

Aamu looked at her dull leaves "Yaa, I miss him too"

Meanwhile, Leera and Silku were returning from the fields with handfuls of yummy cereals."Mom, can we go to Nooppy and Aamu? It has been days since I went there." Leera smiled and agreed. She saw two men coming to Caseu on a motorcycle. They walked to the backyard talking and laughing loudly. They reached Nooppy before the tiny squirrels. Seeing them there, the mom-son duo took a detour to the right for the guava tree. Silku is still unaware of the danger looming on Nooppy. Those men had an AXE!!

One guy rested the axe on Nooppy and sat down to smoke. He lit a cigarette and in no time the air smelled of smoke. With the puffed up energy spike, the guy walked around Nooppy checking the nearby plants and trees. Nooppy stood frozen in shock. She knew her time was near. Sensing her distress, the leaves lost their grip and started shedding in bunches. Aamu was still in shock. The guy cut all the short, low branches with a big knife. He balanced himself by the roots and raised the axe up in the air for the first cut on Nooppy.

"AAAAHHH.."

He screamed in pain, dropping the axe down. It was a long nail, all rusted thrust up his feet. The other guy tried to pull the nail out, in vain.

Nooppy skipped a heartbeat. She was still in disbelief of what just happened. She thanked the nail many, many times. "Oh my Goodness! That nail!! It lay down here in my shade for so long. Was it waiting here all this time to save me? Was it destined before that this nail would save me from the axe? See the irony here. This man came to cut me down. Now, he is in pain and leaning on me for support." Though she hated him at the very last minute, she tried her best to sway and relax his pain. "After all, we trees are never meant to harm anyone. We never complain about the hottest summers, the heavy downpours or the coldest winters."

Aamu felt a bit relaxed when the guys walked away to get the nail out. Leera hopped on Aamu from nowhere. Aamu told her about the guys, the nail and everything that happened there. Leera felt sad and happy at the same time. Silku bounced on Aamu. Leera signalled him to stop. He now knows the exact reasons for Nooppy's sadness. He tried to cheer her up. But she couldn't come out of her pain that easily. He went to the front porch to check on the two guys. He saw them going out of Caseu on the motorcycle.

On the way back to Nooppy, he glanced into the air-hole for the lizard. "Why is he always sitting inside the house? Why can't he enjoy the beautiful nature outside sometimes? Or, would it be in any danger like the roach said?" His urge to go inside Caseu became stronger. He hoped the net on the air-hole had a hole for him to sneak inside and see the monsters in Caseu.

Silku gave the collected peapods to Leera. He reached the pond. It has been days, he saw Freyu.

"I am sure Freyu would be mad at me for not going there

these many days. The issue is I have to come to the pond even if she wants to see me or I want to see her. She can't come out of the water. He waited at the pond for a long time, but no fish came to see him. He got bored and slid on the palm leaf many times to kill time.

"What happened to Freyu? Is she in danger too? Many kids are here with fishing hooks now, more than before. Fishma always tells Freyu to be extra careful around humans. But, it's Freyu! She never listens to anyone. Hope she is safe. Maybe she is just busy with her friends underwater. It's too hot today, all the fish might be just staying cool underwater."

He waited for Eleema too for a while. But Eleema was also not there near the pond then. Silku returned from the pond, bored. "It's not only the inside of Caseu that is dangerous. Outside world also has dangers hiding in each step. So much to learn about living." His head hurt with stress.

He wished to eat some papaya to calm down. At the papaya tree, the papayas were all covered with nets just like rambutan. "Aah, these unkind humans!" Suddenly he was angry at everyone. Leera was surprised to see her son angry. "Aww, my sweet little boy is all grown up. He has started to react to unjust things."

"My dear son, anger is not at all a solution for life. Life just unfolds differently for everyone. It's those people's papaya. They would do anything to guard it. You should control your anger. See, we have so much other food for us. Go and find some other food." He replied with a mean stare. "How could my Mom be so tough sometimes?" Leera sensed his frustration. "I miss my sweet son. He used to listen to whatever I told him before. He never questioned me. He didn't argue with me about anything. He was so happy, so active playing on all the trees without any worries. How soon did that sweet boy evolve into a mature young adult" Leera sighed.

Aamu showed Leera the axe still leaning onto Nooppy.

"It's not over yet, Leera. See the axe is still there. They might come back anytime. I just can't think of Nooppy's state now. She will be screaming of pain inside. That axe there is just like cancer eating you up alive." Aamu whispered so Nooppy wouldn't hear.

"How I wish I could grab that axe from there and throw it away into space or the sea!" Aamu was too emotional.

The 'Axe-war'

The days are usually darker at this time of the year. A raincloud loomed over the sky, all the time, to pounce down in a jiffy.

Rain or shine, Aamu was worried about the axe on Nooppy. She asked each and everyone for a way out of this issue. No one had an answer. All the fire ants at Caseu, united as an army, tried to pull the axe away from Nooppy. The axe was too heavy for them. It didn't move an inch.

"It's not that we were so confident of our strength. It's just out of love. After all, it's our Nooppy." The fire-ant chief commander, Puttare, balanced himself on the lone leaf and discussed the 'axe-war' strategies with Aamu.

"I really don't know how long..but I am sure, we lived on her from ages back. First it was only you, Aamu. Do you remember the first colonies we made ? And that time, when those stupid parasites were all over you. It was us who attacked and defeated them. It's because of us, you had mangoes that year, that too, tons of mangoes. I think we were mostly here. Then Nooppy came along. She grew up in no time. She didn't need much of our help, but. Now, I understand that insects or parasites were always less or not at all there on Nooppy. Maybe she was not healthy from the beginning itself. Nooppy was never like other plants or trees. Most of the trees or plants get an insect bite or infection in a season.

We are naturally trained to attack those insects. Nooppy never had such conditions."

"If we knew before, like when the guys were here with the axe, we could have attacked them then and there itself. You know, Aamu, as the elders say, prevention is better than cure, maybe not always, but most of the time."

Fire-ants are always busy building up colonies. They just don't concentrate at a single location. They spread the queen's eggs in many nearby areas, then build up the colonies at each location. So they have one place or the other, even if something terrible happens at a place. Puttare, like most of the fire-ants, hated to brood over some matter and leave the daily chores unfinished. He silently marched into his day.

" How could I tell her not to be depressed? It's just not a passing phase. It's death for her, 'THE END' for her" Aamu looked at Nooppy in sympathy.

"It's ok, Aamu. Each tree has its own destiny. It's just fate." Nooppy stuttered over a sad grin. Aamu felt Nooppy's strength to be strange. "Maybe she just accepted the situation. She might be preparing herself for the end." Aamu shivered with just that one thought.

A light breeze passed Caseu. It paused a bit longer at Nooppy and caressed her gently.

Nooppy went back in time, when she was a happy sapling in the small pot at the nursery. It was so fun. Lots of similar sprouts in a huge pot. A friendly breeze stayed at the nursery all day long.The nursery always had many people there to buy seeds, plants, pots, plant food etc. Kids run through the rows of pots while adults select their pet-plants. The owner was crazy about plants and always had thousands of plant varieties in the nursery.

The Grandma loved little Nooppy at first sight. "It's not always that we get a tree with both beautiful fragrant flowers and sweet fruits. Nooppy is one such special tree. " She didn't believe the owner's words at first. He added " See, the flowers of mango, apple and even papaya! And think of those fruits.. Nooppy has both. " Grandma promised to get Nooppy the next time. He didn't force her to buy either. Nooppy and her friends became hopeful whenever someone came to the nursery. They were outgrowing the small pots very fast. Grandma came to the nursery deciding to get Nooppy home. But she realised the re-planting would be best just before the rainy season. She left the nursery without the tree that time too. Nooppy and her friends were fed up with the congested small pots. The roots were all crumbled up and there was not enough water and food for any of them. But they are plants and patience is their virtue. Nooppy and her friends waited patiently for bigger pots and loving new owners.

But the nursery owner had to immediately sell off the nursery. He walked all through the nursery to wave adieu to all his lovely plants one last time. Nooppy and all other plants at the nursery were devastated at this change. Call it a lucky streak for Nooppy! Reaching home, the owner felt that Grandma would never get Nooppy plants once he left the nursery for good. The next day he took all the Nooppy saplings and went in search of Grandma's home. Grandma was excited to get this many Nooppy plants.

Grandma, the sweetest lady in town, distributed all the saplings except one to her friends & family. She picked the best sapling for Caseu and planted it before the rainy season set in. She took care of Nooppy as a baby. With good food, lots of water, ample sunshine and rain, Nooppy grew into the beautiful, shady tree.

Thinking of Grandma, the nursery and the little Nooppy, Nooppy felt sad all the way more than before.

Rain is Here..

The earth stayed humid as if in a furnace. People wished a cloud would pass by in the next moment and drench them in happiness.

Finally, one day, it rained..

The rain gently mended the cracks in the parched earth. The dried trees got elated and jived into the rhythm of the rain. The earthly scent after the rain is so magical! It leaves any soul afresh. Every being at Caseu peeped out of the rain shelters to savour the petrichor. Silku glanced at the moist and all the way prettier Caseu. It never ever had any moldy patches or green moss growing on the walls. The house stayed warm & white all through the seasons.

It seems, the occasional summer showers are not enough to clean off the world. The first rain of the majestic rainy season is only strong enough to just wash off the summer debris. Is it the raindrops bouncing at earth's every loud laugh or is it that the earth is laughing hard seeing the naughty, bubbly drops? Ah! The rain and the Earth – their eternal true love for each other never ceases!

The yearly maintenance works started at Caseu after the first rain. The twigs and branches got pruned and the new saplings were planted for the optimum growth at the proper time. The lotuses in the semi-pond waltzed in the rain. The lotus leaves couldn't contain the excitement of the raindrops.

The raindrops tapped and tapped on the leaves and splashed onto the fish there.

The frogs came out of their houses and croaked in ecstasy. They literally melted into the puddles. The termites on Aamu couldn't brave the rain and they got swept off with the first rain.

In the rain, Nooppy smiled after a long time. Her leaves murmured and shared the happiness too.

Into the Future

Nature was all cheered up for the fiesta. It's the time for harvest after the rains.

The sun showed up again after continuous cloudy days. The rivers gushed in abundance, caressing the spring-laden banks. The weaver birds' were back at their weaving and the nests-in-progress fluttered on the coconut trees. The weeds tangled their tiny, cute flowers with the twigs on ground, thus kissing life back into them. Even the tiniest of the grasses were blessed with flowers through the rainy season.

Caseu's garden appeared to be a fabulously colorful flower rug.

The flowers attracted butterflies and bees with their colors or fragrances. All the beautiful bugs spread love being the messengers of nature. The flowers always gift the sweetest nectar to the beetles & bees as a token of love for sprinkling their pollen for the future generations to come.

The ever-active honey bees collect the honey to feed everyone in the hive and save the unused honey for later.

One day, Silku passed by Blacky's cage. The vines all over her kennel were full of beautiful flowers. "Are those flowers or butterflies?!" He got confused.

He whistled at Freaky just to annoy her and reached the security's room. He noticed a bunch of peanuts in that room yesterday. He peeked in through the window. "Yesss…the peanuts are still there…buuuttt, it's too far…" Silku wrecked his brain.

The security reached there with an axe on his shoulder. Silku saw two little leaves on it and felt a shiver passing up his spine. It was Nooppy's leaves. "Nooppy laying down on the ground, lifeless, cut right at the roots…" Silku shut his eyes tight to erase that painful thought.

Silku cried out high & loud for Leera from the rambutan tree. He wanted to tell Leera all about Nooppy. Leera was on the papaya tree near the outhouse, enjoying a ripe papaya all by herself. Hearing Silku's cry, Leera wished to reach Silku in no time. She saw him running towards Nooppy and she sprinted there too. "Thank God, at least he's safe!!!" Leera murmured.

When Leera reached Nooppy, Silku was swinging merrily on Nooppy. "What's the matter, Silku?"He didn't answer. He jumped onto Aamu. Leera noticed some peanuts below Nooppy. She hopped onto them and then she knew it." The axe is not there. It's gone.``Leaving the peanuts, Leera ran to the tallest branch of Nooppy and hugged her tight. Nooppy was elated and swayed merrily along with Leera. Some yellow leaves fell from her onto the ground and Leera shouted " Happy leaves …it's just the happy leaves". Nooppy laughed out loud.

"But, why did Silku cry?" Leera couldn't shrug off her thoughts. She noticed her friends once more. "Aamu is happy. Nooppy is happy too. But is she really happy? Is she just faking her happiness?" She saw Silku playing on the plantain leaves. He seemed to be relaxed, though.

The paddy fields out there were getting mature day-by-day. Nature was getting ready for the harvest.

Nooppy was watching a sparrow getting all the twigs, grass and yarn-bits to build a sweet nest.``It's the boy sparrow's duty to build the nest.." Aamu shared her gyan. "Hmm…yeah..he tried to build one on the front window yesterday. Someone came and tore it out. Hope he could finish building this and live in there too.." Nooppy hoped good for the lil bird. " Do not worry, Nooppy. The birds are made for all these. They go through the hurdles all the time. But it's always good at the end. They build the coziest nests and lay the eggs, hatch them and train their little ones. Everyone - birds, animals, people all want to provide the best for their little ones. It is the cycle of life." Nooppy smiled " Aamu is always so optimistic. She always thinks of only happy endings!What she said is true..Everyone wishes for the life buzzing all around them, always. Like me, all the trees would wish for flowers, bees and butterflies through all the seasons." She sighed and dreamt of a bloomful future.

A castle, but Dark..

Caseu was getting ready for some big celebration. Cars, that too foreign brands, were flowing in and out of Caseu all the time. Nooppy could always sense the preparations. She gets excited too with all the hustle & bustle.

A couple of workers came by Nooppy , measured the space around her and did some calculations. The next day, two awnings were raised in front of Caseu - one small & one big. People flocked in and Nooppy soaked in all the cheer, even though a silent anxious ache throbbed through her veins. Aamu, being her bestie, could sense her anxiety. In quiet consoling strokes, Aamu tried to relax Nooppy. In the breeze, Aamu hugged Nooppy evenmore. Nooppy felt at ease and loved Aamu for being there for her through her tough times.

The guests at Caseu celebrated life loud with all of the universe's music, dance and food. Nooppy got a share of the feast too. Silku, as always, got scared of the loud humans and hence stayed away from them. Blackie and Freakie were always trained to keep mum in the crowds. Even the minutest being in Caseu's yard cooperated with the humans during the celebration. In his new set of uniform, the security was unusually busy boasting about his duties.

Evading the crowd, Silku reached the rear sunshade to get hold of his new curiosity - the coldest little lizard. "He might be knowing what exactly is going on inside the Caseu. But, will he talk to me today? Or at least look at me…After all, in this big wide world why would he behave like this , that too, to the tiniest me? Maybe because he lived his whole life inside the house. One should venture out in nature to enjoy the beautiful things around. Look at me..I have lived all my life out in the nature and how wise I turned out to be.." He felt a halo lit up around his head and he beamed with pride.

The celebrations did not cease at night either. Caseu was still bursting high at moonrise. The kitchen and bathroom drains were busy all through the night.

Leera peeped at Caseu in the dawn hours and noticed Caseu hasn't shut down yet. "If things are this busy inside Caseu, it means by now Nooppy would be drenched in water from there. With lots of water, why would Nooppy still be sad? Is she being too hard on herself? If she is healthy as she seems to be, will they cut her? Why would people decide to cut an otherwise healthy tree? Who would know all the answers?.. Someone from inside or someone who knows what's going on in there?..The crow! No..she has no interest to talk about these things. .. and she might be hating those insideCaseu. Whenever she is near the house to get some food, they will come out of nowhere and shoo it away. So mean!!!..Hmm.. The parrot might know..Noo..she never goes near the house. Blackie would be a good source. But, will he open up to me? He seems to be the owner's favourite. He would not spill the secrets, if any. After all, what does he do? He just gobbles up what is fed and snores loud all day. I don't even want to talk to him. Aah, yes..Eleema! She might not know what's going on inside Caseu, but she might have an idea to know the insider story. She would be ready to help too..Won't she?" Leera strolled through the farms and fields looking for Eleema. Not seeing Eleema anywhere, Leera got frustrated. " How could Eleema know all these..Silly me! TA-DAA!! The mice family living in the outhouse might know."

Leera was getting impatient on the rambutan tree. She tried to slide through the window panes in the outhouse. She saw a mouse laying there on a sack with about a dozen teeny-tiny mice. She has not seen this mouse before. The mama-mouse was scared for her tiny battalion and got alert. Seeing Leera, she felt relieved and was ready to listen to her too. But she didn't have any answers. " I never went in there. Aah, right.. now I remember, sometime back I had a friend from inside there. But, we never talked about Caseu. I haven't seen her for a long time now. Dont know what kind of world is inside there." She went back to her miniatures.

Leera went to Nooppy and sat staring at Caseu . Silku saw Leera on Nooppy and came running to his Mom. Leera sighed and mumbled out all her fears.

The duo looked onto Caseu and it grew big and dark on them – A big, dark castle of secrets!

Krish - The Hero

After the monsoon harvest, cattle were all over the fields. Cranes visited the fields in flocks. Occasional drizzles were still happening now and then even through the brightest of the days of the season.

Caseu has been unusually quiet for some days now. Silku felt as if something unfamiliar was about to happen at Caseu." Why does the security always sleep these days? He doesn't have any work, it seems. Blackie is also silent. He is also sleeping through the day. Haven't seen Freaky for quite some days now. No one to be afraid of ..It feels so good to be free to roam around as much as I want."

But somewhere in his mind he was scared to be very much free too.

Nooppy was staring at the closed windows of the somewhat still Caseu. The breeze stayed for some time at her, but she didn't care to even sway to its tunes.

Aamu could senseNooppy's despair at seeing Caseu all locked up and silent. Aamu had her own doubts. " Why is she always overthinking stuff? Life happens. Life will keep on happening. It's the rule of nature. The show has to go on. There could be no pause for either summer or winter. Neither Spring nor the rains wait for cheerleaders..They just arrive on their own. When the entire universe can evolve to the seasons, why can't a small, simple tree like Nooppy follow the rules of life? Why does Nooppy have to resist the flow of life?" But Aamu kept these questions to herself as she didn't want to make Nooppy sad anymore.

Nooppy could read Aamu's mind. "Knowing I am disturbed, Aamu is not talking to me as usual. That's so unlike of her. Isn't it our duty to be loyal to our owners? Shouldn't we become the shade for them? What will humans do without the plants & trees around? Am I thinking too much about all these? How can someone senior like Aamu not think of any of these? Or is it that she has given up on her life?" She was getting too emotional.

Silku came to Nooppy with a new friend. Aamu was amused to see him enjoying the newfound freedom at Caseu. They hopped on Nooppy and Aamu. But his friend didn't like to hop onto Nooppy and back. Nooppy didn't have anything to munch on. Silku never cared about it. When he is full, he just loves to bounce on both Nooppy and Aamu. Both of them couldn't even miss him for a single day. And if Leera is there, it's a lot more merrier. Two more friends came to Nooppy searching for Silku. Nooppy was slowly getting distracted from all of her worries.

Silku heard an unusual howl from Blackie when he was playing with his friends on the outhouse roof. He looked down and saw a big, fat snake slithering behind Blackie's house. The security came running at Blackie's alarming howl, but the snake had disappeared into nowhere. "How did the snake know that Caseu is closed? No one is in there to harm him? Will there be more creatures coming into Caseu ? Are we not safe here anymore?" He was puzzled.

Silku forgot about the empty Caseu for a while. One day, he saw that mysterious lizard at the sunshade. He had slid himself out more than usual. To Silku's surprise, the lizard didn't ignore him as before. He didn't even retract back into his eternal cave. Silku stared into that tiny being. He was sure something monstrous was hiding in Caseu. He felt that the lizard could be a part of that monstrous gang. He casually waited there to see the lizard's next moves. He moved closer to him and waved a short 'Hi'. The lizard seemed to be friendly today. He slid out a bit more into the sunlight. Silku encouraged him. "Ohh..he has grown fat..no wonder, he cannot come out of that tiny hole."

"Come buddy, let's go play,"Silku shouted. The lizard was not interested in becoming instant buddies. He didn't want to play at that moment, for sure.

He gave a cold shoulder to the play invite. "I am Krish.." he introduced himself.

"Kkkrriisshh…!!!" Silku repeated the name in wonder. " How could one have such a funky name?"

Krish started to brag. " There is a picture of GOD inside the Caseu. I stay behind that picture. Most of the time, the people there would come in front of the picture and shout Krishna, Krishna especially when they are going out, they have some important event and things like that. Do you know, it's me who takes care of Caseu when they go out. So to be trendy, I just shortened Krishna as Krish.."

"Hmm..have heard of something called God. But, Krishna!!..what is that? Who is that? " Silku didn't want to believe anything that he just heard. " How can someone tiny like you manage this big house? Dude, how do you do that?"

Krish continued his bragging. "When no one is there, I come out from the back of the photo. My family and friends come out at that time, too. We feast on the food spills on the floor." He emphasised " Now no one is there. The full responsibility of Caseu is on my shoulders now."

Silku was eager to know about an all-together different world inside the Caseu. He didn't want to believe half of the things Krish said. The secrets at Caseu were still at large.

He interrupted." Yaa, where did everyone go?"

"They went on a foreign tour." Krish said in a casual tone.

"Foreign?" Silku's eyes and mouth were wide open with questions.

"Ohh, u dont know what foreign is? Ok, I'll tell you..that and many more things." Krish put his teaching cape on.

Silku got bored of Krish's class. He wandered along on the sunshade as if he was listening, he silently escaped from there and landed on Nooppy.

Krish was irritated. " This is the dumbest squirrel I have ever seen. He didn't listen to a single word I said. Silly one." He went back inside the window in disbelief.

Mystery Unfolds..

Silku went in search of Leera. He wanted to tell Mom about everything Krish told him. He spotted Leera and his new friend on a tree far away and he shouted for her. Leera decided to meet Krish and know more details about Caseu.

Leera scanned Kris from head-to-toe. Leera has seen the lizards on the trees before. But, the ones that stay inside the house."Is he different from the lizard that stays outside?They seem to be pretty much the same. No matter where they live, the lizards are not at all beautiful creatures. How can they have no fur? Or did someone remove all the fur on them? Eyes, ears, nose ..that all are similar like us. Do they stick the tummy onto the floor? Why do they do that? How can they move then? Anyways, Silku is smart. He found a lizard from inside the house and made his friend to explore. What all he cannot do? My silly boy!!"

Krish started his virtual Caseu tour for the mom-son duo." There is a thing called TV in all the rooms. You can see anything-n-everything on that. Sometimes it is all about God, sometimes it's fashion. There are funny things and emotional ones too. My favourite is the food one - they call it the cookery show. Some like the cinema and some the series shows. But the one which is most watched is 'The Animal Planet' . That's how I know about most of the animals and nature."

Leera couldn't grasp many of the things. But she didn't

show her dislike. She waited for the part with the Caseu secrets to start sooner.

Krish was beaming with pride in his new role. He felt Leera and Silku respect him a lot and he couldn't suppress his excitement. He tried to slide himself more out into the sunlight to talk clearly.

"THHUUDD!!!" Something big fell in between them and they all scattered away. Leera braved out from the corner and scanned the thing. It was just a piece of coconut. The crow was passing by and he might have lost his grip. She couldn't stop laughing thinking how they got scared and ran away. She came back to the window. Krish was nowhere to be seen. Leera went closer and looked at something there. "Oh, Oh no..it's a tail..its Krish's tail.." she screamed at Silku. "The coconut fell on Krish and chopped off his tail. But, where did he go? Leera and Silku looked everywhere. "There, he is … Krish is there!" Leera shouted pointing at a pale and shivering Krish sitting inside the window.

Krish came out of his safe haven. He looked at the tail on the floor. "This is actually our trade secret. " Looking into Leera's doubtful eyes , he continued "Yaa, we use this to escape from our enemies."

"Enemy?! What is that? " She stopped her question. She didn't want Krish to think she is stupid. "Anyways, it's not me nor Silku. We are not anyone's enemies ."Leera's focus shifted onto Krish's movements. "Krish can move on the walls so swiftly. We use the hind legs to find balance to move on the trees. Are the lizards on the trees different from us too? "

Someone moved near the hole in the window. Krish looked back and introduced her "This is my wife!""WIFEEE?1?.. Now what's that? " Leera was all the more confused. "Is Krish someone like us or is he a human? Maybe because he lives inside the house, he is copying whatever the humans do." Krish went back inside Caseu with his wife.

Alberto and Puttero were on Aamu, listening to every minute details Leera procured from Krish. The crow was there on Aamu too. She was never back at Aamu once her nest was empty. "Aamu never has fruits for me. Then why should I waste my time coming here? Today just rested for a bit when passing by and the conference started below. Gossips and rumours are always fun. Yaa..I know Caseu is empty for awhile. I don't think they know about the other thing yet. Some grand ceremony is about to happen at Caseu. They will not know this from me, for sure. Let the spies go and find out on their own. Leera and Silku are always on Aamu and Nooppy and they can closely watch Caseu from here. Even then they couldn't find about this? Thats strange! Hmm..they are not crows, right. They lack our vision too..Can't help..Poor fellows!" The crow flew away from Aamu.

Aamu frowned her lips seeing the crow flying away in the middle of the meeting. "She is always like that. When she needs something, she will be here. She comes to me to build the nest, to lay eggs. I have to go through all those loud caws day and night. Then she goes without any thanks. When I have fruits, she will be here out of nowhere. No fruits, she will ignore me just like that! How rude.. The crows!! '' Aamu clenched her teeth. " They have very much unity among themselves. I am sure of that. They always roam around in flocks. If one of them is in danger, they call out for help and the whole flock would be there in no time to save the friend. They are usually very intelligent. They know humans more than any of us. I am sure she knows what is happening inside Caseu more than us, but will not help us. "

"One thing is clear now. Something's not right in Caseu. That is being drained out into Nooppy too. No wonder why her fruits are not as tasty as before. Root is our main part. Root sends the food and energy to all of our other parts. If the root itself is being targeted, how can a tree stay healthy? Being a fellow-tree, I can understand Nooppy and her worries.

No other squirrel, ant or bird will be able to ever understand what is happening with her." Aamu's voice trembled in grief.

"I had a doubt about the health of Nooppy's roots. That's why asked Alberto to build the ant colony there. As he said no to it, it's clear that the problem is at the roots itself. Puttaro refused to go inside Caseu. He says he and his friends cannot stand the strong pungent smell in there. How to stop all this craziness? No matter what, I should be with Nooppy. I should do everything possible to save her." Aamu decided.

"I am just a tree. I can't move around and check what's happening in and around Caseu. I know Leera and Silku are trying their best to help us out. But they are squirrels after all. They have impatient genes. Spywork needs lots of patience. That they don't know. The best person is the crow. But alas!she flew away without saying anything. '' Aamu drowned in her own thoughts.

Leera repeated her findings to Puttaro and Alberto. "Krish mentioned that lots of strong, harmful chemicals and lotions are being used there." They didn't know what to do and hence kept quiet. Aamu felt proud of Leera for taking the initiative to save Nooppy. She was happy to get a smart assistant like Leera for the 'Save Nooppy' mission.

Nooppy silently listened to all the conversations and discussions. Knowing her stress, her friends didn't include her in the discussion. Nooppy could sense that Caseu is empty. Her roots were dry for the last two days. Though she felt a bit dehydrated, she was relieved that she didn't have to drink up all the tasteless & harmful chemicals.

Freyu, Smart as Ever..

Silku had to share all the new information with Freyu. Earlier, he could slide through a bent tree branch and reach the pond. It was cut during the rains. Silku explored and found a new wooden bridge to reach the pond. The pond was calm as usual. Silku noticed that there are very few fish in the water now. Where did all the fish go?

Seeing Silku at the pond, Freyu swam towards him underwater and jumped high up near him. He was startled to see the loud ripple sound. He was happy to meet her after a long time. She seems to have put on weight and there was a bulge in her tummy. What did she eat this much? Or is it just water in her tummy?

Freyu was happy to meet Silku too, but she was not as loud as before. She tried to act mature. She told him it's all eggs in her tummy and not some food or water. He didn't want to believe his friend grew up so much. He opened up to her about all the happenings at Caseu, meeting Krish and everything going around him. She was eager to know about all the new things too.

"Why don't you go inside Caseu and see for yourself what is happening inside?" .

"How can I go in there? Silly girl..The doors and even the windows are all closed." Silku didn't want to continue the stupid chat.

"Ey..Silku..The house is now in Krish's control, right..So if he is your friend, can't you go inside?"

Silku's eyes twinkled. "That's a good idea. Why didn't I think about this earlier?" He looked at her in awe. He wished that she lived on the land instead of water, so he could have company for all the investigations.

"When will you be laying the eggs?" He changed the topic. He didn't want her to think as someone silly. She ignored the question as she herself didn't have an answer for it.

Silku waited for Fishma for sometime, but was not able to see her. Meanwhile, he saw some new fish at the pond. Some of them already knew him. He grew impatient and left for Caseu. His mind was fully focused to get into Caseu somehow. There should be a solid plan to go in and come out of the house safely. "Maybe Ratma could help. She, Ratus and all other rats are experts in digging holes through the walls. She would know, for sure. Or should I ask Krish first and then ask Ratma for help. Or should I discuss all these with Mom? But, when will I be able to tell her all these? She is always busy with her new friend." Silku's head spinned with thoughts and questions.

"Maybe there is a way to get inside the house from the roof. It's better I go alone and check for a way to get inside. If someone comes with me, they might also wish to get inside. Then chances are more likely to be caught. No..It's not safe. Going alone is the best option." Silku finally decided to meet Krish and make a plan for the 'Mission Caseu'.

Silku waited for Krish near the window for a long time. It was too dark inside the window and so he couldn't see if Krish was in there or not.He had stored a cereal grain in his cheek to give Krish as a token of friendship.

"I would give the cereal first and then tell him about the plan to go inside Caseu. If he says no, I can tell him about Eleema. She would dig underground holes and take me there.

What if he says no then? Ohh, should I save the cereal till he approves the plan and agrees to take me in? Or would I lose the cereal for nothing?"

Krish didn't come out that day. Silku went on the roof and saw many other friends having fun there. All of them went to Nooppy and played on her till evening,

Nooppy was too happy to have Silku and his friends on her. She always noticed that Silku and all his friends are always gentle on her. They never pull out the leaves and do any harm to her. She told herself these are the beautiful little nothings that would add up as happiness in her life.

Aamu was a bit relieved too, seeingNooppy happy with Silku. Aamu noticed that Nooppy has grown a bit big and looks prettier now. She has stopped leaning onto Caseu lately and is slowly coming out of the loneliness too.

Krish Goes Missing..

Silku was getting worried for Krish. He was trying to get hold of Krish for some days now, but he is nowhere to be seen. He is not there even at his regular place.

"What could have happened to him? Why is something always spooky about the inside of Caseu? Why can't it be as beautiful as it is outside? If the people left Caseu under his control, would they try to harm him?"

Silku went to the front porch. Blackie was sleeping in his kennel, as always. Or maybe he is just relaxing with eyes closed. Silku then headed to Freaky's kennel. Two chameleons were there on the plants near Freaky's kennel. He always gets amused looking at them and how they change their colour. "One day, even the security couldn't spot the chamaeleon on the plant. They just camouflage into the surroundings and lay there with their tongues sticking out. All the time, the little bugs are the ones who get trapped. How are they able to do that? It's such a cool trick. If I had that, I wouldn't have to hop on all the trees and collect food. One time, I was digging a hole under the teak tree to store the grains. There were some eggs under the soil. Mom said those are the eggs of these chameleons and not to harm them. I put the soil exactly as it was as she told me. How can someone be so irresponsible and leave the eggs underground? What can I say ..it's how they are made and who can change the ways of nature"

Silku remembered Krish and went back onto the sunshade. This time too, he wasn't lucky. Krish was still hiding in the dark, cold Caseu. When he was on the sunshade, Alberto and his army were busy marching away with Krish's tailpiece and Silku somehow missed the scene from the top.

Silku was about to go onto Nooppy, but instead he went on to the rose-apple tree on the other side. Sometimes, he could see the inside of the house from that tree. He just wanted to try that way now just to make sure Krish is safe there. When he was watching Caseu from there, he saw Leera and her friend going onto the rambutan tree. He was happy that Leera got a new friend and she is happy. But, sometimes, he misses the sweet times with his Mom, hopping together onto trees and sharing all the new and exotic tastes together.

Mission Caseu

Silku had no interest in doing anything. He wished to meet Krish and get into Caseu really bad. But Krish is nowhere to be seen, and doesn't feel like sharing these with Mom - Silku was feeling really low. He had decided he'll meet Freyu with the hot, breaking news from the insides of Caseu only. So he can't go to the pond and meet her either.

Silku had been waiting for Krish for sometime now. He had the grain of cereal for Krish today too. Today seems to be lucky for him. Krish appeared after a while at the window. Krish was friendly this time. He waved at Silku. "Long time, buddy…where were you?"With the cereal in his mouth, Silku couldn't start chattering. He waited for Krish to come out of the window to him. Krish didn't move from the window. Silku finally took the cereal grain out and put it on the floor for Krish to see. "See, this I brought for you."

"What is that?"Krish got curious.

"It's a gift for you. It's a grain of cereal. It's really yummy."

Krish burst out laughing. "I don't eat this kind of stuff. My favourites are something made of milk, butter and those kinds of things. It's not that I don't eat any other things. I do eat other things , sometimes."

"Milk, butter - Now, what are these??Everytime I meet him, he would say something new. When will I learn all of these things? This is getting tougher. " Silku sighed out loud.

"Krish, you are so lucky!"

Krish pushed his tummy up from the floor "Why do you say so?"

"See, you are living inside such a big house. And they love you, trust you so much. They have asked you to guard Caseu in their absence, right. You are so lucky."

Krish felt very much privileged.

Silku added "Krish, I really want to see the inside of Caseu. Would you help me with that?"Krish didn't expect that at all. He couldn't deny Silku's wish too. "Silku, my dear friend. Ofcourse I will help you. Today it's not possible. How about after two days? Is that ok for you?"

Silku was getting ready to plead more for the Caseu tour. He was surprised Krish agreed to it so easily. He got excited. He stood tall on his hind legs."You come here at this same spot at this same time after two days. Let me find a way for you to get in by that time."

Silku felt so proud of himself. But he decided he'll not share this with anyone, not even to Mom. He was waiting for Krish for a long time and now he felt hungry. He still had the grain of cereal with him. But he then felt like having papaya to celebrate the moment. He hopped onto the mangostein tree from the guava tree. On the way to the papaya tree, he spotted Leera on the outhouse roof. To safeguard his secret, he ignored Leera and went straight to his sweet destination.

Krish had a different thought. "Silku thinks very highly of me. He feels I am somebody great in Caseu. I should do something to bring him here." He looked all around Caseu for a way to bring his friend inside.

The Royal Caseu Tour

The third day, Silku was there at the planned spot on time. Krish appeared at the window a little later. He came out through the hole and moved towards Silku. Silku then noticed that Krish doesn't have his tail. But he didn't want to annoy Krish with silly questions.

"All the doors and windows are closed tightly. But, there is a small way through the kitchen. You can come in through there." Krish's voice was stern.

"Hmm..But I don't know where this thing called kitchen is? And how to find out the way in there?" Silku was losing hope.

Krish offered to go with him towards the kitchen area. Silku hopped with excitement through the sunshade. Krish was more cautious. He slid through the wall hiding himself from all the preying monster birds. Silku was amazed to see Krish's skill to move up and down the walls. Again, he didn't want to shift the focus from the mission. After a sharp right turn from the sunshade, there were lots of twists and turns. Silku had never seen this part of Caseu. Silku jumped after Krish through a ring. Something was spinning in there. He was careful to jump through the spinning blades.

"Jump…" Krish shouted and Silku jumped. He had no clue where he landed. It was pitch dark in there.

"You stay there, Silku '' He could hear Krish through the dark too. Silku couldn't balance himself very well there. There

was a strange smell in there too. He started to feel suffocated..
No air, no light. He felt claustrophobic.

"Come, let's move" Krish's next order. "To where?" Silku's
voice was shaky.

Silku saw light streaks here and there. He started to feel
a bit safe.

"See, this is the kitchen. Look up here. This is where we
came in. This machine is called the exhaust fan. "

"Machine…" Silku echoed the word in his mind.

"This will push all the air inside to outside, But there is
one thing, it must be switched on" Krish's lecture was getting
tougher to grasp.

Even though he didn't understand all the things Krish said,
Silku started to analyse his surroundings. He looked around
the place called the kitchen. What all things are there on the
walls. It looks just like a wonderland. And here on the floor,
there are no rocks, no stones, not even a single grass. Maybe
that's why it's too slippery here.

"This is a thing called glass. In that shelf, it is the plates,
bowls and all." Silku's mouth opened wider and wider.

The next room was bigger. Krish didn't stop there. He went
to another room and Silku followed him. That room had the
same four walls around it, But the floor was different. It was
not slippery any more. But Silku's sharp claws got stuck in
the soft yarns.

Krish jumped onto something. "This is called a sofa. If
someone comes from outside, they sit here. This part, where
I sit right now, is where they keep their hands on. Silku, you
also jump and sit on this."

In no time, Silku jumped onto it and sat on it. He didn't
like it though. "Nooppy or Aamu is so much better than this
to sit. Sunshade or the riverside is better than this too. How
do people sit on this?"

Krish was at the tallest part of the sofa. They could see each other very well now. Silku felt Krish is so smart to choose the right spot on the sofa.

Silku wanted to jump upon the sofa. Krish resumed his tour then." That's AC. It's too cold when it starts working. All the others are light bulbs. The one high up here is the fan. It will spin and make a cool breeze all around the room."

Silku didn't see any of these - He didn't see the AC, the fan or the lights. He realised one thing. THERE'S NO SKY HERE!

He couldn't digest the fact. " So is there no day and night here? Where will it rain from? How do they get water? " Silku felt he was going to faint at a place with no sky.

"One Grandpa, one Grandma, one Dad, one Mom and their three children.. All of them stay here..I wanted to show you the bedrooms too..but they are all locked.." Krish was all into being a tour guide.

Silku didn't listen to half of Krish's speech. He was ecstatic in the newfound wonderland. "Hmm..Something is missing. I don't feel good here..Is it because Mom is not here? Eey.. Mom and me are not together all the time like before. But, yaa ..I miss her now..I miss Mom, my friends, Nooppy, Aamu, Freyu…What is in a world for me without all of them?"

Krish got down from the sofa and went somewhere. Silku got scared. "I shouldn't have come here. I knew some danger was here.. I was right too. I shouldn't have listened to Freyu. I am hungry.." He felt like crying being all alone in the horrifying world.

After some time, Krish came and took Silku to another room. There was a shelf open up on the wall. Krish went inside and motioned Silku to jump along. Silku jumped with his full might, he landed with a thud and slipped some of the bottles down. Silku was terrified and he ran away from there. Krish couldn't stop laughing seeing Silku run for his life.

Krish slid down from the almirah. There were some peanuts on the floor scattered from one of the broken bottles. Krish asked Silku to try the peanuts. There was some honey dripping from another bottle. Krish told Silku to taste that too. Silku was an expert at sucking up the nectarine from the banana flower, but he didn't know how to drink up the honey from the floor.

Munching onto the peanut, Silku told Krish " I have to leave.""Why? What happened?Didn't you like this place? Krish was surprised to hear Silku wants to leave so soon.

Krish wanted Silku to stay back a little longer. " Do you know I feel so lucky to be born here. My wife is also here. She is sleeping now. Usually, we both sleep during the day. We are awake at night. We eat food mostly at night. Today, I am awake now for you."Silku felt thankful to Krish for being such a sincere friend.

"Do you know there are TV, AC in all the rooms? You can get to know about all the happenings around the world through the TV."Silku was not at all interested in the machines inside Caseu. He tried to lick a bit of the honey from the floor.

"Silku, everyone here in the house went for a foreign trip. They will be back after three or four months. Silku munched upon the peanuts one after another. He didn't listen to Krish at all.

Krish licked some honey with his tongue-tip and slid up the wall. He sat midway on the wall and asked Silku to come up there. Silku jumped up there. Krish tried to open something. Silku helped him to turn it round and round. Water gushed out from the tap. Silku was happy to see water as he was feeling too thirsty after reaching inside Caseu. But, he found it too tough to drink water flowing out of the tap.

"This is the tap. When we turn it round and round like how we did, water will gush out of it."

"Ohh..now things are getting clear. Inside the Caseu is not like outside. Nothing is free here. Humans use machines to get everything. They have one machine for the air, another one for the cold air, one for the water and things like that. Aah.. so did the peanuts and honey come out of the machine too? But that machine is broken now." Silku got his facts clear as Krish went on mumbling about Caseu.

All of a sudden, Silku saw that!" What is this?Who is this? Krish said only he and his wife are here. Maybe there are other lizards too. But this?!!!"

Silku was frozen with fear. He regretted his decision to come inside Caseu once again."How did this happen? Did this come out of a machine too?" He felt a loud cry choking him up. He wanted to see Mom then and there.

Krish jumped upon Silku from nowhere. Silku screamed out loud.

"Hey, be cool, Silku..You don't have to be scared. That is a mirror. It's you in there. You are seeing yourself there, my friend!"

"Hmm…Another machine!" Silku relaxed a bit. "The security has a machine, light comes out of it. There is another one to get water from the well. Oh yeah..there is one more to cut Nooppy These crazy humans, their life is always after one or other machines, it seems."

Silku posed himself in different styles in front of the mirror. He felt amused looking at himself like that.He couldn't stop looking at the three stripes on his back. He had always wondered if he had those stripes like all other squirrels. Krish also enjoyed Silku's modelling session. He laughed out loud and went back to the tap.

Krish and Silku tried to close the tap, in vain. Water didn't stop gushing out. "See Silku, this is called washbasin. Do you see the white ball in there?" It reminded him of the chameleon's egg he found under the tree and he was about to say it out loud. Krish interrupted. " Those balls are used so roaches will not enter the Caseu through the drain. It is poison for the roaches."

"Ohh..so what the roaches said was right..there is poison here to kill them. Now, the secrets are unfolding one by one. I am sure, there are more secrets in here. It might be in those locked rooms. Let it stay locked forever. Will I also die like that roach if I go and open those doors now?" Silku was scared for his life.

Krish moved ahead and yawned in between.

"It's ok, Krish..now you can go and sleep. I will leave now and come back sometime later."

Krish didn't agree to it. "That'll not work out, buddy. Anyways, you are here. You stay with me for two or three days. Now, it's almost one month since these people left for their trip. The security will be coming with the cleaning disinfectants anytime soon. They are too harsh and have a strong smell. Once the cleaning is done, I will pass out for days. I was knocked out for four continuous days last time. "

Silku wanted to run from there at that moment. He was no more curious about Caseu. He didn't want to see anything more. He came back to the kitchen. He saw Alberto's army marching up there. They are coming from Aamu's roots. But how could they get in? Silku looked for the ant's secret tunnel in the kitchen. Krish joined him " There are no disinfectants on the floor now. It has been a long time since the floors have been cleaned. That's why the ants are able to come here… me too"

Silku could guess that. The ants were so reluctant to come inside Caseu some days back. Silku had smelled something strange when he stepped inside the kitchen. That smell is still there. Maybe the ants and Krish got used to the smell. Silku came to a conclusion. He felt proud of himself for exploring so much hidden information. Silku and Krish toured through Caseu for a little more time.

The Big Reveal

Aamu was standing still with her thinking cap on. Nooppy seemed to be relaxed these days.

They have not seen Silku for the last couple of days. Both of them missed him badly. They have known Silku from the time he was a baby. Both of them watched how he grew up. Silku always loved to play on Nooppy and Aamu no matter the season. He was a regular on both the trees. Leera was confident he would be with one of his friends and will be back soon.

Some of Silku's friends came searching for him. They waited at Caseu's roof, then came to Nooppy. They hopped between Nooppy and Aamu for some time. There was nothing much to do for them. There were no fruits on both of the trees too. They left after a while.

It was a foggy day. "Alberto seems to be busy for the last two or three days. They were inside Caseu. He told me two or more colonies got enough food for sometime, He is an efficient leader." Aamu told Nooppy. Nooppy agreed. "They could get in when the house is empty. Now there is no one to use the chemicals. So it would be easy for them. "Collecting the last bits of crumbles from all over the Caseu, Alberto and his army marched out of the house through a window crack.

Silku woke up after a long slumber. He was hungry and thirsty. He couldn't remember how long he had been sleeping.

" Yes..I went inside Caseu. Where is Krish? " He tried to call out loud for Krish. But he couldn't speak. He wanted to move. But he wasn't able to move either. He lay down there hoping for some help.

Krish came to him sometime later. "Do you remember I showed you a bottle of that harmful chemical? I told you not to go near it. Did you listen? You went near it, touched it and the bottle fell down. And then the chemical spread all over here. You slipped in that lotion and you fainted right in it."

Silku thought he was so lucky to be reborn in Caseu.

Some water drops fell on his face. He felt he got some energy now. He sat up. "Aaha..it was Krish who operated this machine and got me water. He is great. He has learnt so many things staying inside here with the intelligent people. If he was as big as them, he would have also built many more machines like this. He is a genius!"

Silku was getting hungry as hell. "The yummiest papaya and guava, the crunchy cocoa pods.." Haa, Silku couldn't resist his hunger anymore. "Have to get out of here soon. But I need some food before that." He looked for the peanuts from the other day. But, Alberto and his friends had snatched all the peanuts from the floor.

"Wait, I will find a way for you to go out. You can come back later sometime. These people will take more time to be back. Now the water is flowing out through the tap, right. So the tank above will be empty soon. The security will come to check where the water is leaking from. So now you have to leave Silku. Aah..One more thing. There is some grand celebration going to happen in this house. They went abroad to do the shopping for the same. Once they are back, the wedding will happen soon. And your Nooppy! It didn't have any fruit on it for a long time now. So they might cut it and build something there for the wedding. You should come back once more before they are back. We just covered half of Caseu.

There is lot more for you to see and learn." Krish was still excited that he could bring Silku inside the house.

Silku was shattered to hear the news. He forgot his hunger and everything. What he and everyone else feared about, it's going to happen. Nooppy will be no more.

Thunder rumbled outside. It started to drizzle. Silku decided he will not be back inside the house anymore. He didn't tell Krish about that. But he decided in his mind enough is enough. He climbed upon the gas cylinder, then onto the tube and then through the exhaust fan wire onto the exhaust fan. As before, he jumped out through the blades. He didn't even want to look back into the house. Anyways, it's too dark in there, he would not be able to see Krish from here.

When he reached the sunshade, Krish was there at his usual spot. The rain got heavy by then. Silku couldn't move away from the sunshade. He stood there thinking about Nooppy. Krish watched Silku and continued his gyan. "Silku, The chemicals from the house all go to Nooppy. You also know it. Nooppy's fruits lost taste because of that. Over time, Nooppy's health deteriorated and she will not have fruits anymore."

Silku could feel a loud cry brewing from his inside. He wanted to save Nooppy, but didn't know how!

Winter

Silku enjoyed his freedom to the fullest once he was out of Caseu. He had his favourite papaya, guava and all other food he got hold of, like there is no tomorrow.

He rushed to meet Freyu and shared all the tid-bits from the Caseu. Freyu wouldn't believe what she heard.. A world without any rivers, lakes or even water..not even fish! Why don't they make a machine for fish too just like the machine for water, the peanuts and the honey? Will there be any trees inside the house ever? Will there be any lake or river ever in there? What kind of world is that?

Silku shared the dark fate waiting for Nooppy, only to Aamu secretly. "I knew this was gonna happen" Aamu sighed. Leera was not interested in Silku's well being anymore. She stopped caring for him altogether. He noticed a small bump on Mom's tummy and he knew the matter very soon.

Silku met Krish at the sunshade and they had their casual chit-chat.

"Aaha, your tail is back. How did it happen?" Krish didn't understand Silku's excitement. "What is in there? It usually grows just like that."

It was getting colder outside. Dewdrops were there on all the leaves in the mornings. Some trees lost their leaves too. Stars in different shapes and colours were hung outside the security's office. There were stars outside most other homes too. Days went by faster.

Some new blooms appeared on Aamu. She was getting herself ready for the fruiting season ahead. Silku was going to the front porch through Nooppy one day. He met Krish at the window. Krish came out through the window. "It's almost time for the Caseu people to be back. Don't know the exact date. But they will be back anytime now." Krish didn't finish his sentence.

Silku was not at all concerned about the Caseu people not back yet. He was busy with his new girlfriend. He was on his way to hang out with her and other friends on the rambutan tree. Krish had gauged Silku before. He knew he wouldn't care much about the owner's return.

A Pandemic

Silku went to the river with Mayu, his new friend. They met Freyu there. Freyu has the second set of eggs in her tummy. When it's time to lay the eggs, she'll find a safe place. She will not stay back to take care of the kids. The offspring are on their own from day one. Some other fish guard the eggs till they hatch. They will take care of the little ones till they are fully grown. Sometimes, if some other big fish attacks them the mama fish will hide the baby fish in her mouth and protect them from danger.

Mayu liked the river side. She roamed around the river. Silku thought about Eleema and Ratus when he was there at the river side. It had been a long time since he saw both of them.

Silku told Freyu that the people at Caseu are not back yet, but will reach anytime now.

"Eey, Silku..so didn't you know? Those who went abroad, will not be able to come back now. There is some pandemic going on. So people cannot travel. It will take a long time for them to be back."

Silku wondered about Freyu's general knowledge. He was startled to the core, but didn't show it outside. "How did you know all this?"

"The people who came to the pond were talking about this yesterday. I heard it from them." Freyu was proud of her general knowledge too.

"A pandemic is something which spreads to a large number of people from a small group of people. It might be tough to contain it in one place, so the authorities in each country will take required measures to control the spread. Hence the people are not allowed to travel."

This was something new for Silku. Where would the people at Caseu be now? Where did they go? Is that place too far? How far will that place be from the corn fields? The people are experts in making machines for each and everything. Will they be able to build a machine for this pandemic too?

Mayu came to Silku after exploring the pond and nearby area. Silku waved bye to Freyu and left for Caseu with Mayu. Freyu went underwater with her friends.

Caseu was impatient waiting for its owners. The nature outside Caseu was dull too. The flowers in the garden bloomed at its time, the butterflies feasted on them as usual with no worries of the pandemic. The bushes grew out wild and untamed. Algae formed in the water fountain on the front porch. The reptiles and other creatures got the land back from the busy humans and enjoyed the newfound freedom. All the trees and plants at Caseu became ecstatic during that time of the year.

The Happy Nooppy

It was almost afternoon, Silku took Mayu to his drey. He had plans to renovate his house. He wanted to put new twigs and freshen it up.

But as soon as he reached his home, he saw it! Leera lying down with her new baby squirrels!!

"Mom's new kits!" He said in his mind. He left the nest with Mayu.

There was no end of surprises for him that day. The next surprise was Nooppy. There were new leaves on her. Then he saw the new branches and at last he saw what he was waiting for a long time, little flower buds on Nooppy!

Silku couldn't contain his happiness. Silku and Mayu hopped on Nooppy and laughed out loud. They then reached Aamu.

Seeing everyone's excitement, Nooppy got cautious" I am happy too.. but, these buds should stay, they should grow, bees and butterflies should come and germinate."

Aamu had her share of happiness too - baby mangoes were all over her.

Days didn't wait for anyone. The buds blossomed into big beautiful flowers. Nooppy looked elegant as if wearing a flower crown. The fragrance of the pink flowers conquered Caseu in no time. The bees and butterflies couldn't resist the temptation at all. They buzzed in and around Nooppy all the time.

Aamu hugged Nooppy tight.

Silku and Mayu joined them in a warm, cosy group hug.

www.ingramcontent.com/pod-product-compliance
Lightning Source LLC
LaVergne TN
LVHW041746190726
843493LV00008B/2470